This Water Polo Notebook Belongs To

Thank you for your purchase.

This journal has been created especially for Water Polo players and coaches.

Hope you enjoy using this for all your exciting and thrilling matches.

If you like this, please share your feedback. Your Amazon rating and review will help us reach more players, coaches and will also help us improve.

Thanks Again!

Copyright © 2021 Aaron Smyth
All rights reserved. Contents of this book may not be reproduced, duplicated or transmitted without permission from the author or publisher.

GAME/ STRATEGY NOTES

GAME/ STRATEGY NOTES

GAME/ STRATEGY NOTES

GAME/ STRATEGY NOTES

GAME/ STRATEGY NOTES

GAME/ STRATEGY NOTES

GAME/ STRATEGY NOTES

GAME/ STRATEGY NOTES

GAME/ STRATEGY NOTES

GAME/ STRATEGY NOTES

GAME/ STRATEGY NOTES

GAME/ STRATEGY NOTES

GAME/ STRATEGY NOTES

GAME/ STRATEGY NOTES

GAME/ STRATEGY NOTES

GAME/ STRATEGY NOTES

GAME/ STRATEGY NOTES

GAME/ STRATEGY NOTES

GAME/ STRATEGY NOTES

GAME/ STRATEGY NOTES

GAME/ STRATEGY NOTES

GAME/ STRATEGY NOTES

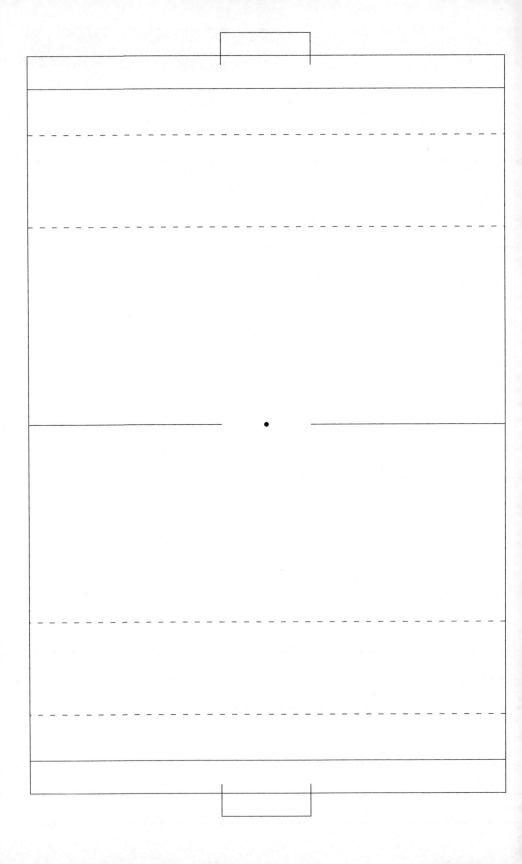

GAME/ STRATEGY NOTES

GAME/ STRATEGY NOTES

GAME/ STRATEGY NOTES

GAME/ STRATEGY NOTES

GAME/ STRATEGY NOTES

GAME/ STRATEGY NOTES

GAME/ STRATEGY NOTES

GAME/ STRATEGY NOTES

GAME/ STRATEGY NOTES

GAME/ STRATEGY NOTES

GAME/ STRATEGY NOTES

GAME/ STRATEGY NOTES

GAME/ STRATEGY NOTES

GAME/ STRATEGY NOTES

GAME/ STRATEGY NOTES

GAME/ STRATEGY NOTES

GAME/ STRATEGY NOTES

GAME/ STRATEGY NOTES

GAME/ STRATEGY NOTES

GAME/ STRATEGY NOTES

GAME/ STRATEGY NOTES

GAME/ STRATEGY NOTES

GAME/ STRATEGY NOTES

GAME/ STRATEGY NOTES

GAME/ STRATEGY NOTES

GAME/ STRATEGY NOTES

GAME/ STRATEGY NOTES

GAME/ STRATEGY NOTES

GAME/ STRATEGY NOTES

GAME/ STRATEGY NOTES

Printed in Great Britain
by Amazon